What Is Clean Energy?

Defining the Prob

Lela Lawson

COMPUTER SCIENCE For the REAL World™

Rosen Classroom™

Published in 2018 by The Rosen Publishing Group, Inc.
29 East 21st Street, New York, NY 10010

Book Design: Jennifer Ryder-Talbot
Editor: Caitie McAneney

Photo Credits: Cover RFarrarons/Shutterstock.com; p. 4-5 vladimir salman/Shutterstock.com; p. 4 (hazard icon), 20 (recycle icon) EveeKamp/Shutterstock.com; p. 7 Naypong/Shutterstock.com; p. 7, 12, 16 (leaf icon), 8, 15, 18 (electric icon), 11 (sun icon) A_KUDR/Shutterstock.com; p. 8 Calavision/Shutterstock.com; p. 10-11 amophoto_au/Shutterstock.com; p. 12 SasPartout/Shutterstock.com; p. 15 CrackerClips Stock Media/Shutterstock.com; p. 16-17 N.Minton/Shutterstock.com; p. 18 tchara/Shutterstock.com; p. 21 Atsushi Hirao/Shutterstock.com.

Library of Congree Cataloging-in-Publication Data

Names: Lawson, Lela.
Title: What Is clean energy?: defining the problem / Lela Lawson.
Description: New York : Rosen Classroom, 2018. | Series: Computer Kids: Powered by Computational Thinking | Includes glossary and index.
Identifiers: LCCN ISBN 9781508137894 (pbk.) | ISBN 9781538324448 (library bound) | ISBN 9781538353271 (6pack) | ISBN 9781538352953 (ebook)
Subjects: LCSH: Renewable energy sources--Juvenile literature. | Clean energy industries--Juvenile literature.
Classification: LCC TJ808.2 L39 2018 | DDC 333.79'4--dc23

Manufactured in the United States of America

CPSIA Compliance Information: Batch #WS18RC: For Further Information contact Rosen Publishing, New York, New York at 1-800-237-9932

Table of Contents

A Big Problem

Think about all the things we do that rely on electricity. We watch TV, play video games, use the computer, and turn on lights in every room we enter. Unfortunately, creating electricity is often harmful to Earth. The more we use, the more of an effect we have on the **environment**.

You can see the harmful clouds of pollution coming out of a factory.

Most electricity is made by burning **fossil fuels**. Coal is burned in factories to make steam that spins a **turbine** and creates electricity. Unfortunately, burning fossil fuels is not good for Earth.

Clean Energy Solutions

Fossil fuels are nonrenewable, which means they will run out someday. They are sometimes taken from Earth in harmful ways. When they are burned, they harm the **atmosphere** and create pollution. This is a big problem!

Luckily, people have developed clean energy sources as a solution. Clean energy sources are renewable, which means they will not run out. They also don't pose a risk to Earth or create pollution. Read on to learn more about how clean energy can solve the problem!

Engineers have spent years coming up with solutions to the fossil fuel problem.

These wind turbines are high in the mountains.

Energy from Wind

Have you ever seen a wind turbine? These huge machines usually have a tall pole and three long blades. When it's windy, the blades turn. This makes motion energy. A **generator** inside the turbine turns this energy into electricity.

Earth will always have wind. That means wind energy is renewable. Some power companies build wind farms with many turbines. They can supply electricity to many people. One of the largest wind farms in California has more than 4,800 wind turbines!

Energy from the Sun

The sun sends energy to Earth in the form of sunlight. If you've ever touched a car on a sunny day, you can see how sunlight turns into heat energy. People also build glass structures called greenhouses that let in a lot of sunshine and keep the structure warm.

Sunlight can also be turned into electricity if you have a generator. People use solar panels to turn sunlight into electricity. These long, flat machines are a great source of clean energy in areas that get a lot of sunlight.

The sun gives energy to plants to grow. Everything on Earth exists because of sunlight.

Adding solar panels to your house is a great way to cut down on nonrenewable energy use.

Solar Panels

How do solar panels work? People place them in areas that get a lot of direct sun, like a roof. Then, they hook up the solar panels to a system that powers the house.

Some people use solar panels to power their own house. They join solar panels to their main power system. Other people connect their solar panels to a larger **electrical grid**. The panels can power their house, and if they make enough electricity, it can be used to power other houses as well.

Energy from Water

Electricity can be made from water using hydropower. Hydropower works a lot like wind power. Moving water, like moving air, is used to turn turbines. The turbines generate electricity.

People have been using hydropower for electricity since the 1880s. It was becoming very popular until World War II, when coal mostly replaced it again. Like most clean energy sources, hydropower is renewable because water will always flow. Rushing water turns the turbines. People build dams to control the amount of flowing water.

These are the turbines inside the power plant at the Hoover Dam. Each year, the Hoover Dam gives electricity to **8** million people.

Geothermal Power

Geothermal energy comes from inside Earth. The layer underneath Earth's surface is hot, and can heat up underground stores of water. We can see this with hot springs, which are small bodies of water heated by underground **volcanic** activity.

You can see the steam rising from this geothermal power station.

People use geothermal energy to both heat and cool their homes. They can also use it to make electricity. Power plants can use underground steam to work a generator. This is most common in places with many hot **reservoirs**.

Leftover wood can be made into pellets and burned as fuel.

What's Biomass?

Biomass energy is electricity made from burning natural **materials**. Natural materials include trees, plants, and leftover paper and wood.

Think of a bonfire. People burn wood to let off energy in the form of heat. This energy can also be turned into electricity. Factories that burn coal can instead burn biomass and make steam to run the generators. Other forms of biomass that people burn to create electricity include **manure** and trash. Biomass is a great solution because it uses leftovers and waste to make power.

What Can You Do?

Many of these switches to clean energy need to be made on a larger level. However, there are things that you can do to help, too!

Use less electricity. Buy energy-smart light bulbs, which use less electricity. When you leave a room, make sure you turn off the light. Always turn off the TV and computer when you're done with them. Never leave the refrigerator door open or leave water running. Talk to your parents about putting in solar panels or other clean energy devices.

Don't forget to turn off the light!

Solving the Problem

The problem of fossil fuels won't be solved overnight. We are very dependent on nonrenewable resources and they've been used for a long time. However, there are many renewable and clean sources of energy that can help solve the problem over time.

Solar panels and wind turbines are just two examples of solutions that engineers have created to solve this big problem. Over time, more engineers will invent new **technology** in response to the fossil fuel problem. Do you have any bright ideas?

Glossary

atmosphere: The mixture of gases that surround a planet.

electrical grid: A connected system for delivering electricity from suppliers to users.

engineer: Someone who plans and builds machines.

environment: The natural world.

fossil fuels: Matter formed over millions of years from plant and animal remains that is burned for power.

generator: A machine that uses moving parts to produce electrical energy.

manure: Solid cow waste.

material: Something used to make something else.

reservoir: A place where something is stored, especially water.

technology: The way people do something using tools and the tools that they use.

turbine: A motor operated by the movement of water, steam, or air.

volcanic: Having to do with volcanoes, or openings in a planet's surface through which hot, liquid rock sometimes flows.

Index